750

Daily *warm-ups*

JOURNAL WRITING

J. WESTON
WALCH
PUBLISHER
Portland, Maine

1   2   3   4   5   6   7   8   9   10
ISBN 0-8251-4360-8
Copyright © 2002
J. Weston Walch, Publisher
P.O. Box 658 • Portland, Maine 04104-0658
www.walch.com
Printed in the United States of America

Table of Contents

Introduction *iv*

The *Daily Warm-Ups* series is a wonderful way to turn extra classroom minutes into valuable learning time. The 180 thematically grouped quotations—one for each day of the school year—spark students' critical-thinking skills. These daily quotations may be used at the very beginning of class to get students into learning mode, near the end of class to make good educational use of that transitional time, in the middle of class to shift gears between lessons—or whenever else you have minutes that now go unused. In addition to providing students with structure and focus, they are a natural path to other classroom activities involving critical thinking and writing.

Daily Warm-Ups are easy-to-use reproducibles—simply photocopy the day's quotation and distribute it. Or make a transparency of the quotation and project it on the board. You may want to use the quotations as a take-home assignment to jump-start creative writing. Included in this front matter are suggestions for ways students might respond to the quotations. Or you may use your own writing prompts. These writing activities are a wonderful way to get students to explore their ideas and articulate their thoughts.

However you choose to use them, *Daily Warm-Ups* are a convenient and useful supplement to your regular lesson plans. Make every minute of your class time count!

Ways to **RESPOND**:

Rephrase or restate the quotation in your own words. How is the meaning of the quotation changed by your choice of words?

Explain the quotation. What do you think the author meant? What does the quotation say about the life and personality of the author? What does the quotation mean in your life?

Summarize the quotation. Write a short essay in which you explain why you agree with the thoughts expressed in the quotation. How have your experiences been the same or different from those expressed in the quotation?

Pose questions. What questions does the quotation spark? What questions would you ask the author? What questions about life does the quotation raise for you?

Offer an alternative view. Explain why you disagree with the sentiments expressed in the quotation.

Note your first thoughts when you read the quotation. What images, feelings, or memories does the language evoke? Write a poem with these words that fits the tone and mood of the quotation.

Describe a situation in which this quotation relates to your life.

Challenges

"Every setback is the starting point for a comeback."

—Anonymous

1

Challenges

"I am not afraid of storms for I am learning how to sail my ship."

—Louisa May Alcott

2

Challenges

" If you miss seven balls out of ten, you're batting three hundred, and that's good enough for the Hall of Fame. You can't score if you keep the bat on your shoulder."

—Walter B. Wriston

3

Challenges

" *S*elf-pity in its early stages is as snug as a feather mattress. Only when it hardens does it become uncomfortable."

—Maya Angelou

4

Challenges

"Loss is nothing else but change, and change is nature's delight."

—Marcus Aurelius

5

Courage

" Life is a series of experiences, each one of which makes us bigger, even though it is hard to realize this. For the world was built to develop character, and we must learn that the setbacks and griefs which we endure help us in our marching onward."

—Henry Ford

6

Courage

"**O**bstacles are those frightful things you see when you take your eyes off your goal."

—Henry Ford

Courage

"The greatest test of courage on earth is to bear defeat without losing heart."

—Robert G. Ingersoll

8

Courage

" Life shrinks or expands in proportion to one's courage."

—Anaïs Nin

9

Courage

" It takes a lot of courage to show your dreams to someone else."

—Erma Bombeck

10

Courage

" **I** have learned over the years that when one's mind is made up, this diminishes fear; knowing what must be done does away with fear."

—Rosa Parks

11

"Dare to be yourself."

—André Gide

12

Courage

" Nothing in life is to be feared. It is only to be understood."

—Marie Curie

13

Courage

"Behold the turtle. He makes progress only when he sticks his neck out."

—James Bryant Conant

14

Courage

"Take a chance! All life is a chance. The man who goes furthest is generally the one who is willing to do and dare."

—Dale Carnegie

15

Courage

"**Y**ou must do the thing you think you cannot do."

—Eleanor Roosevelt

16

Courage

Daily Warm-Ups: Journal Writing

"Courage is the power to let go of the familiar."

—Raymond Lindquist

17

Courage

"Courage is the most important of all the virtues, because without courage you can't practice any other virtue consistently. You can practice any virtue erratically, but nothing consistently without courage."

—Maya Angelou

18

Dreams

" Live out of your imagination, not your history."

—Stephen Covey

How does your imagination color your life?

19

Dreams

"**W**hatever you can do or dream you can, begin it. Boldness has genius, power and magic in it."

—Johann Wolfgang von Goethe

20

Dreams

"**K**eep away from people who try to belittle your ambitions. Small people always do that, but the really great make you feel that you, too, can become great."

—Mark Twain

21

Dreams

"It is never too late to be what you might have been."

—George Eliot

22

Dreams

"One can never consent to creep when one feels an impulse to soar."

—Helen Keller

23

Friendship

"A friend is a second self."

—Aristotle

24

Friendship

"It is that my friends have made the story of my life. In a thousand ways they have turned my limitations into beautiful privileges, and enabled me to walk serene and happy in the shadow cast by my deprivation."

—Helen Keller

25

Friendship

"**P**eace is achieved one person at a time, through a series of friendships."

—Fatma Reda

Daily Warm-Ups: Journal Writing

26

Friendship

"My friends are my estate."

—Emily Dickinson

27

Friendship

"The only way to have a friend is to be one."

—Ralph Waldo Emerson

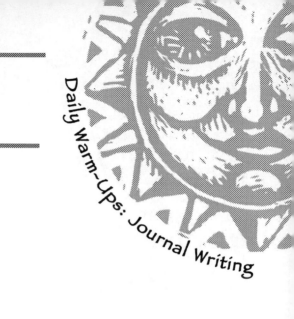

28

Daily Warm-Ups: Journal Writing

"Friendship with oneself is all important, because without it one cannot be friends with anyone else in the world."

—Eleanor Roosevelt

29

Friendship

"Friendship is like money, easier made than kept."

—Samuel Butler

30

Friendship

"A friend is one who knows us, but loves us anyway."

—Fr. Jerome Cummings

31

Friendship

"My best friend is the one who brings out the best in me!"

—Henry Ford

32

Daily Warm-Ups: Journal Writing

Friendship

"A real friend is one who walks in when the rest of the world walks out."

—Walter Winchell

33

Happiness

"Laughter is the shortest distance between two people."

—Victor Borge

Daily Warm-Ups: Journal Writing

34

Daily Warm-Ups: Journal Writing

Happiness

"Worry never robs tomorrow of its sorrow, it only saps today of its joy."

—Leo Buscaglia

35

Happiness

"**W**hoever is happy will make others happy too."

—Anne Frank

36

Happiness

"People are just as happy as they make up their minds to be."

—Abraham Lincoln

Happiness

"To be interested in the changing seasons is a happier state of mind than to be hopelessly in love with spring."

—George Santayana

Daily Warm-Ups: Journal Writing

38

Happiness

"Earth's crammed with heaven."

—Elizabeth Barrett Browning

39

Happiness

"There is no duty we so much underrate as the duty of being happy. By being happy we sow anonymous beliefs upon the world."

—Robert Louis Stevenson

40

"Happiness is not a possession to be prized. It is a quality of thought, a state of mind."

—Daphne du Maurier

41

Happiness

"The excursion is the same when you go looking for your sorrow as when you go looking for your joy."

—Eudora Welty

42

Happiness

"Happiness is inward, and not outward; and so, it does not depend on what we have, but on what we are."

—Henry Van Dyke

Hope

"Hope costs nothing."

—Colette

44

Hope

" If you keep on saying things are going to be bad,
you have a good chance of becoming a prophet."

—Isaac Bashevis Singer

45

Ideas

"Knowledge is power."

—Francis Bacon

46

Ideas

"Borrowed thoughts, like borrowed money, only show the poverty of the borrower."

—Marguerite Gardiner

47

Ideas

"Prejudices, it is well known, are most difficult to eradicate from the heart whose soil has never been loosened or fertilized by education: they grow there, firm as weeds among stones."

—Charlotte Brontë

Do you think education could be the key to opening people's hearts and minds? Why or why not?

48

Ideas

"Minds are like parachutes—they only function when open."

—Thomas Dewar

49

"Prejudice is the child of ignorance."

—William Hazlitt

50

Ideas

"The empires of the future are the empires of the mind."

—Winston Churchill

Daily Warm-Ups: Journal Writing

Ideas

"The first problem for all of us, men and women, is not to learn, but to unlearn."

—Gloria Steinem

52

Ideas

" A new idea is delicate. It can be killed by a sneer or a yawn; it can be stabbed to death by a joke or worried to death by a frown on the right person's brow."

—Charles Brower

53

Ideas

" **I** can't understand why people are frightened of new ideas. I'm frightened of the old ones."

—John Cage

54

Ideas

"It is not good enough to have a good mind; the main thing is to use it well."

—René Descartes

"**B**abies of all nations are alike until adults teach them."

—Maureen Applegate

56

Ideas

"Television: chewing gum for the eyes."

—Frank Lloyd Wright

57

Ideas

"Our major obligation is not to mistake slogans for solutions."

—Edward R. Murrow

58

Ideas

"I am enough of an artist to draw freely upon my imagination. Imagination is more important than knowledge. Knowledge is limited. Imagination encircles the world."

—Albert Einstein

59

Ideas

"There are no days in life so memorable as those which vibrated to some stroke of the imagination."

—Ralph Waldo Emerson

60

Ideas

"There's a saying among prospectors: 'Go out looking for one thing, and that's all you'll ever find.'"

—Robert Flaherty

Ideas

"Man's mind stretched to a new idea never goes back to its original dimensions."

—Oliver Wendell Holmes

62

Daily Warm-Ups: Journal Writing

Ideas

"There is one thing stronger than all the armies in the world; and that is an idea whose time has come."

—Victor Hugo

63

Ideas

"If everybody is thinking alike, then somebody isn't thinking."

—George S. Patton Jr.

64

Ideas

"The eyes are not responsible when the mind does the seeing."

—Publilius Syrus

Ideas

"Discovery consists of looking at the same thing as everyone else does and thinking something different."

—Albert Szent-Györgyi

66

"Do you know what individuality is? . . . Consciousness of will. To be conscious that you have a will and can act."

—Katherine Mansfield

Individuality

" Adventure can be an end in itself. Self-discovery is the secret ingredient that fuels daring."

—Grace Lichtenstein

68

Individuality

"There is no support so strong as the strength that enables one to stand alone."

—Ellen Glasgow

69

Individuality

"To have one's individuality completely ignored is like being pushed quite out of life, like being blown out as one blows out a light."

—Evelyn Scott

70

Individuality

"*U*se what talents you have; the woods would have little music if no birds sang their song except those who sang best."

—Rev. Oliver G. Wilson

71

Inspiration

"**M**otivation will almost always beat mere talent."

—Norman R. Augustine

72

"**I**magination is the highest kite one can fly."

—Lauren Bacall

Inspiration

"**W**hen people show you who they are, believe them."

—Maya Angelou

74

Inspiration

"**W**hat lies behind us and what lies before us are tiny matters compared to what lies within us."

—Ralph Waldo Emerson

75

Inspiration

"Everyone has the power for greatness, not for fame but greatness, because greatness is determined by service."

—Martin Luther King Jr.

76

Daily Warm-Ups: Journal Writing

Inspiration

"The key is to keep company only with people who uplift you, whose presence calls forth your best."

—Epictetus

"Obstacles cannot crush me. Every obstacle yields to stern resolve. He who is fixed to a star does not change his mind."

—Leonardo da Vinci

78

Daily Warm-Ups: Journal Writing

Inspiration

"Not knowing when the dawn will come, I open
every door."

—Emily Dickinson

Inspiration

"Genius is 99 percent perspiration and 1 percent inspiration."

—Thomas Edison

80

Inspiration

"There are two ways of spreading light: to be the candle or the mirror that reflects it."

—Edith Wharton

81

"Nothing great was ever achieved without enthusiasm."

—Ralph Waldo Emerson

82

The Journey

"Do not go where the path may lead, go instead where there is no path and leave a trail."

—Ralph Waldo Emerson

83

The Journey

"It doesn't matter where you come from, it's where you're going that's important."

—Anonymous

84

The Journey

"The world is round and the place which may seem like the end may also be the beginning."

—Ivy Baker Priest

85

The Journey

"The secret of getting ahead is getting started."

—Sally Berger

86

The Journey

"He who would travel happily must travel lightly."

—Antoine de Saint-Exupéry

87

The Journey

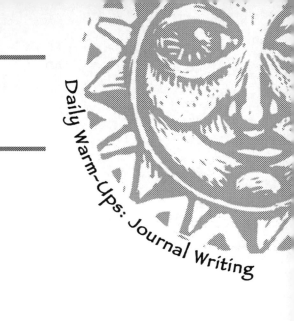

"The beginning is always today."

—Mary Wollstonecraft

88

Daily Warm-Ups: Journal Writing

The Journey

"The journey, not the arrival, matters."

—Michel de Montaigne

89

The Journey

"**I** have always grown from my problems and challenges, from the things that don't work out, that's when I've really learned."

—Carol Burnett

90

The Journey

" Living the past is a dull and lonely business;
looking back strains the neck muscles, causing
you to bump into people not going your way."

—Edna Ferber

The Journey

"You can't step in the same river twice. Each time it is different, and so are you."

—Alice Walker

92

Daily Warm-Ups: Journal Writing

The Journey

"It isn't the great big pleasures that count the most; it's making a big deal out of the little ones."

—Jean Webster

93

The Journey

"**Y**our opponent, in the end, is never really the player on the other side of the net, or the swimmer in the next lane, or the team on the other side of the field, or even the bar you must high-jump. Your opponent is yourself, your negative internal voices, your level of determination."

—Grace Lichtenstein

94

The Journey

"It's not the load that breaks you down, it's the way you carry it."

—Lena Horne

95

The Journey

"**W**hat you are now comes from what you have been, and what you will be is what you do now."

—Buddha (Siddhartha Gautama)

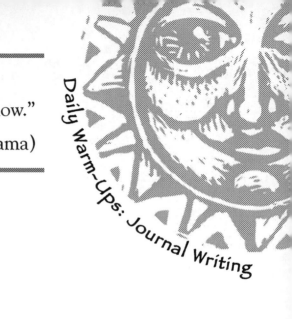

96

The Journey

"The real voyage of discovery consists not in seeking new landscapes but in having new eyes."

—Marcel Proust

The Journey

"The longest journey is the journey inward."

—Dag Hammarskjöld

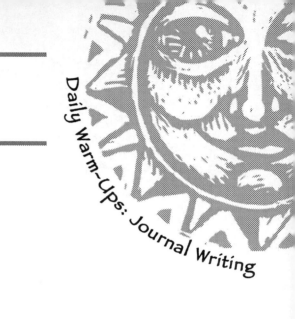

98

Optimism

"**K**eep your face to the sunshine and you cannot see the shadow."

—Helen Keller

99

Optimism

"No pessimist ever discovered the secrets of the stars, or sailed to an uncharted land, or opened a new heaven to the human spirit."

—Helen Keller

100

Daily Warm-Ups: Journal Writing

Optimism

"**W**alls turned sideways are bridges."

—Angela Davis

Optimism

"In the middle of difficulty lies opportunity."

—Albert Einstein

102

Daily Warm-Ups: Journal Writing

Optimism

"A problem is a chance for you to do your best."

—Duke Ellington

103

© 2002 J. Weston Walch, Publisher

Optimism

"The optimist sees opportunity in every danger, the pessimist sees danger in every opportunity."

—Aristotle

104

Proverbs

"One volunteer is better than ten forced men."

—African proverb

105

© 2002 J. Weston Walch, Publisher

Proverbs

"To a mouse, a cat is a lion."

—Albanian proverb

106

Proverbs

"Don't climb a tree to look for fish."

—Chinese proverb

© 2002 J. Weston Walch, Publisher

Proverbs

"**E**nvy eats nothing but its own heart."

—German proverb

108

Proverbs

"To an ant, a few drops of rain is a flood."

—Japanese proverb

Questioning

"Be patient toward all that is unsolved in your heart and try to love the questions themselves."

—Rainer Maria Rilke

110

Questioning

"The power to question is the basis of all human progress."

—Indira Gandhi

Questioning

"There are those who look at things the way they are and ask why . . . I dream of things that never were, and ask why not?"

—Robert F. Kennedy

112

Daily Warm-Ups: Journal Writing

"The only questions that really matter are the ones you ask yourself."

—Ursula K. LeGuin

113

"People are lonely because they build walls instead of bridges."

—Joseph Fort Newton

114

Relationships

"Good fences make good neighbors."

—Robert Frost

115

Relationships

"To understand any living thing you must, so to say, creep within and feel the beating of its heart."

—W. Macneile Dixon

116

Relationships

" As long as you keep a person down, some part of you has to be down there to hold him [or her] down, so it means you cannot soar as you otherwise might."

—Marian Anderson

117

Self-esteem

"I was brought up to believe that how I saw myself was more important than how others saw me."

—Anwar el-Sadat

118

Self-esteem

"To love oneself is the beginning of a life-long romance."

—Oscar Wilde

119

Self-esteem

"There is an applause superior to that of the
multitudes: one's own."

—Elizabeth Elton Smith

120

Daily Warm-Ups: Journal Writing

Self-esteem

"How many cares one loses when one decides not to be something, but to be someone."

—Coco Chanel

121

Self-esteem

"No one can make you feel inferior without your consent."

—Eleanor Roosevelt

Self-esteem

"**W**hether you believe you can do a thing or not,
you are right."

—Henry Ford

123

Self-esteem

"**I** don't think of myself as a poor, deprived ghetto girl who made good. I think of myself as somebody who from an early age knew I was responsible for myself, and I had to make good."

—Oprah Winfrey

124

Self-reliance

"The worst loneliness is not to be comfortable with yourself."

—Mark Twain

125

Self-reliance

"The more faithfully you listen to the voices within you, the better you will hear what is sounding outside."

—Dag Hammarskjöld

126

Self-reliance

"A man has to live with himself, and he should see to it that he always has good company."

—Charles Evans Hughes

"Better keep yourself clean and bright; you are the window through which you must see the world."

—George Bernard Shaw

128

Daily Warm-Ups: Journal Writing

Self-reliance

"The man who goes alone can start today; but he who travels with another must wait till that other is ready."

—Henry David Thoreau

129

Self-reliance

" **I**f you do not tell the truth about yourself you cannot tell it about other people."

—Virginia Woolf

130

Daily Warm-Ups: Journal Writing

Self-reliance

"We are the hero of our own story."

—Mary McCarthy

131

Self-reliance

"There is only one journey. Going inside yourself."

—Rainer Maria Rilke

132

Solitude

"**I** love to be alone. I never found the companion that was so companionable as solitude."

—Henry David Thoreau

Solitude

"No man is an Island, entire of itself; every man is a piece of the Continent, a part of the main . . ."

—John Donne

134

Solitude

Daily Warm-Ups: Journal Writing

"❝ **I** live in that solitude which is painful in youth, but delicious in the years of maturity."

—Albert Einstein

135

Success/Failure

"The only place you find success before work is in the dictionary."

—May V. Smith

136

"*S*uccess supposes endeavor."

—Jane Austen

Success/Failure

"Being powerful is like being a lady. If you have to tell people you are, you aren't."

—Margaret Thatcher

138

Success/Failure

"It had long since come to my attention that people of accomplishment rarely sat back and let things happen to them. They went out and happened to things."

—Elinor Smith

Success/Failure

"There are no secrets to success. It is the result of preparation, hard work, and learning from failure."

—Colin L. Powell

140

Success/Failure

"*S*uccess is to be measured not so much by the position that one has reached in life as by the obstacles which [one] has overcome."

—Booker T. Washington

141

"Destiny is not a matter of chance; but a matter of choice. It is not a thing to be waited for; it is a thing to be achieved."

—William Jennings Bryan

Daily Warm-Ups: Journal Writing

142

"...I have not failed. I've just found 10,000 ways that won't work."

—Thomas Edison

143

Success/Failure

"**I** don't believe in failure. It is not failure if you enjoyed the process."

—Oprah Winfrey

144

Daily Warm-Ups: Journal Writing

"Mistakes are the portals of discovery."

—James Joyce

145

"**S**uccess is a journey, not a destination. The doing is often more important than the outcome."

—Arthur Ashe

Daily Warm-Ups: Journal Writing

146

Success/Failure

" Always bear in mind that your own resolution
    to success is more important than any other
    one thing."

—Abraham Lincoln

147

"Anyone who has never made a mistake has never tried anything new."

—Albert Einstein

148

"The possibility that we may fail in the struggle ought not to deter us from the support of a cause we believe to be just."

—Abraham Lincoln

149

"**W**hat would you attempt if you knew you could not fail?"

—Robert Schuller

150

"Defeat is not the worst of failures. Not to have tried is the true failure."

—George E. Woodberry

151

"Everybody makes mistakes. It's what we make of our mistakes that makes us what we are."

—Anonymous

152

Success/Failure

"Failure is just another way to learn how to do something right."

—Marian Wright Edelman

153

"No one can arrive from being talented alone. God gives talent, work transforms talent into genius."

—Anna Pavlova

154

Success/Failure

"Instead of crying over spilt milk, go milk another cow."

—Anonymous

155

Taking Action

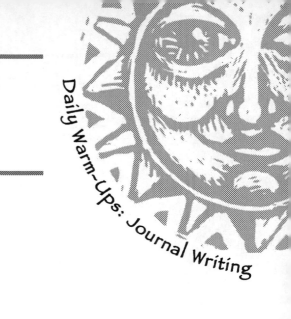

"**M**ost people are more comfortable with old problems than with new solutions."

—Anonymous

Daily Warm-Ups: Journal Writing

156

"Gardens are not made by singing 'Oh, how beautiful!' and sitting in the shade."

—Rudyard Kipling

Taking Action

"**V**itality shows in not only the ability to persist but the ability to start over."

—F. Scott Fitzgerald

158

Taking Action

"You can't build a reputation on what you are going to do."

—Henry Ford

Taking Action

"**W**e must become the change we want to see."

—Mohandas Gandhi

160

Taking Action

"**E**very calling is great when greatly pursued."

—Oliver Wendell Holmes

161

Taking Action

" It's not whether you get knocked down, it's whether you get back up."

—Vince Lombardi

162

"**V**ictory belongs to the most persevering."

—Napoleon Bonaparte

"It is not because things are difficult that we do not dare; it is because we do not dare that they are difficult."

—Lucius Seneca

Daily Warm-Ups: Journal Writing

164

Taking Action

"**E**ven if you're on the right track, you'll get run over if you just sit there."

—Will Rogers

165

Taking Action

> **"W**orrying is like a rocking chair; it gives you something to do, but it doesn't get you anywhere."
>
> —Anonymous

166

"Not everything that is faced can be changed, but nothing can be changed until it is faced."

—James Baldwin

167

Taking Action

"Be like a postage stamp. Stick to one thing until you get there."

—Josh Billings

168

Trust

"Just trust yourself, then you will know how to live."

—Johann Wolfgang von Goethe

169

"The greatest thing in the world is to know how to belong to oneself."

—Michel de Montaigne

170

Trust

"**W**e lie loudest when we lie to ourselves."

—Eric Hoffer

Daily Warm-Ups: Journal Writing

Trust

"It is better to suffer wrong than to do it, and happier to be sometimes cheated than not to trust."

—Samuel Johnson

172

Trust

" Insist on yourself; never imitate. . . . Every great man is unique."

—Ralph Waldo Emerson

173

Wealth

"Measure wealth not by the things you have, but by the things for which you would not take money."

—Anonymous

Daily Warm-Ups: Journal Writing

174

Wealth

"To have and not to give is often worse than to steal."

—Marie Von Ebner-Eschenbach

175

Wealth

"Many wealthy people are little more than janitors of their possessions."

—Frank Lloyd Wright

176

Daily Warm-Ups: Journal Writing

Words

> **"W**e may never know when the right word will transform a person's life."
>
> —Philip White

Words

> " *S*ticks and stones may break our bones, but words will break our hearts."
>
> —Robert Fulghum

178

Words

"Letter-writing is the only device for combining solitude with good company."

—George Gordon, Lord Byron

179

Words

"**W**ords are more powerful than perhaps anyone suspects, and once deeply engraved in a child's mind, they are not easily eradicated."

—May Sarton

180